BOOK 3

Hanon *for* Students

7 Varied Exercises from *The Virtuoso Pianist* for Intermediate Pianists

Edited by
Gayle Kowalchyk
E. L. Lancaster

Alfred Music
P.O. Box 10003
Van Nuys, CA 91410-0003
alfred.com

ISBN-10: 0-7390-8766-5
ISBN-13: 978-0-7390-8766-4

Charles-Louis Hanon

Charles-Louis Hanon (1819–1900) lived most of his life in Boulogne-sur-Mer in France. Born in northern France, the first part of his career (1846–1853) was spent as a church organist and choir director. After leaving the church, Hanon continued to teach voice and piano in Boulogne. He was a devout Catholic and supported the church and its charities throughout his lifetime.

The Virtuoso Pianist

Hanon was a prolific composer writing both teaching pieces and concert music for piano. In addition, he wrote a method for accompanying plainchant, vocal music, an organ method, and a book on harmony. His most enduring work is *The Virtuoso Pianist,* a book of 60 technical exercises that were popular during his lifetime and continue to be used today. It was published in 1873 and won a Silver Medal at the Exposition Universalle in 1878.

About This Book

Hanon for Students, Book 3, contains exercises 14–20 from *The Virtuoso Pianist,* Book 1. In the original version, the exercises were notated in sixteenth notes for two octaves. In this volume, the exercises are notated in eighth notes for one octave so that students may begin to use them effectively at the intermediate level. Each exercise appears five times:

1. with a *legato* touch.
2. with varied articulation.
3. with varied dynamics.
4. with varied rhythm.
5. transposed to A or E-flat. This version can be practiced with the varied articulations, dynamics, and rhythms.

A glossary of one-octave harmonic minor scales is included on pages 37–40.

Practicing Hanon

- Always practice each version hands separately before playing hands together. When practicing hands together, listen carefully to make sure the hands play exactly together.

- A technical suggestion for each exercise is shown on the page with version 1. Technical features also are pointed out in the music.

- First practice slowly, then gradually increase the tempo.

While Hanon exercises can be practiced in a variety of additional ways, the suggestions in *Hanon for Students,* Book 3, promote musical playing as well as technical security.

Technique	Articulation	Dynamics	Rhythm	Transposition

- RH: When *ascending* (mm. 1–7), gently contract the hand between fingers 4 and 1. When *descending* (mm. 8–15), gently contract the hand between fingers 1 and 3.
- LH: When *ascending* (mm. 1–7), gently contract the hand between fingers 1 and 3. When *descending* (mm. 8–15), gently contract the hand between fingers 4 and 1.
- Gently rock the hand and wrist using a small motion on beats 2 and 3 of each measure.

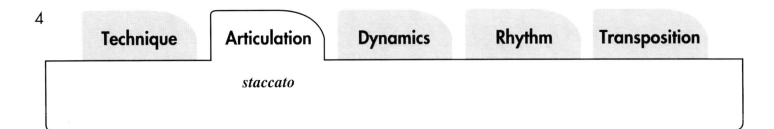

Technique | Articulation | Dynamics | Rhythm | Transposition

staccato

Technique	Articulation	Dynamics	Rhythm	Transposition

crescendo
diminuendo

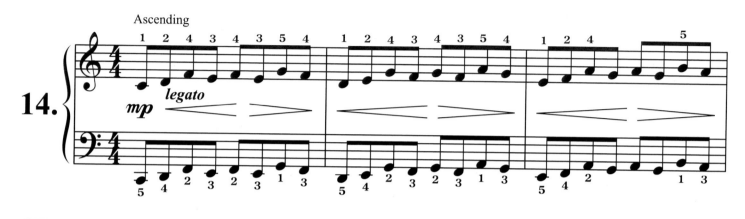

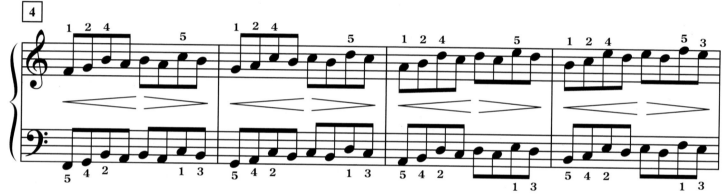

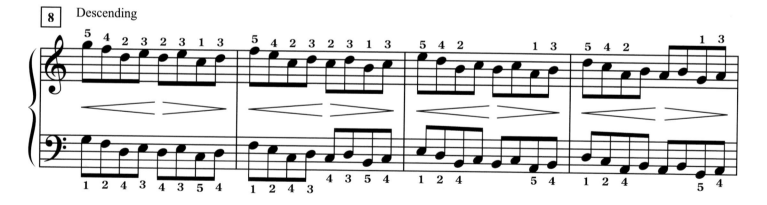

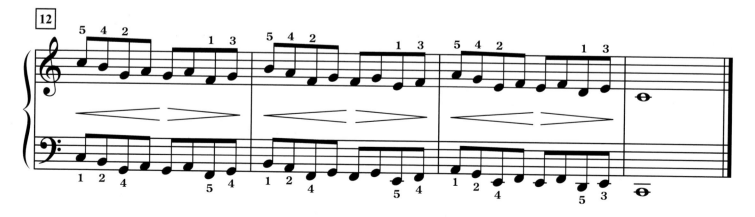

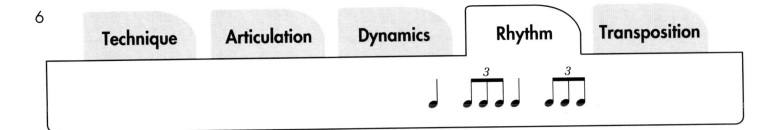

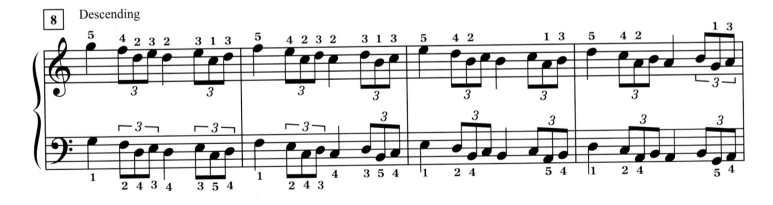

Key of E-flat Major
Remember B-flat, E-flat, and A-flat.

14.

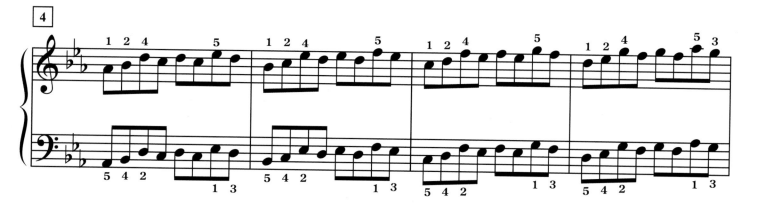

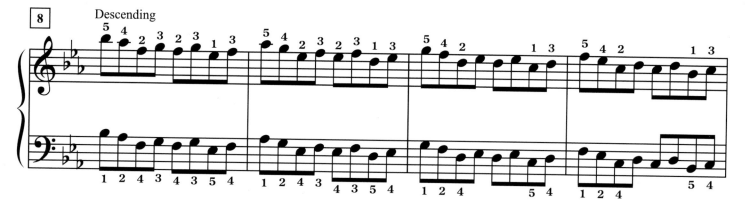

Technique | Articulation | Dynamics | Rhythm | Transposition

- Gently stretch between fingers 1 and 2 and fingers 2 and 1.

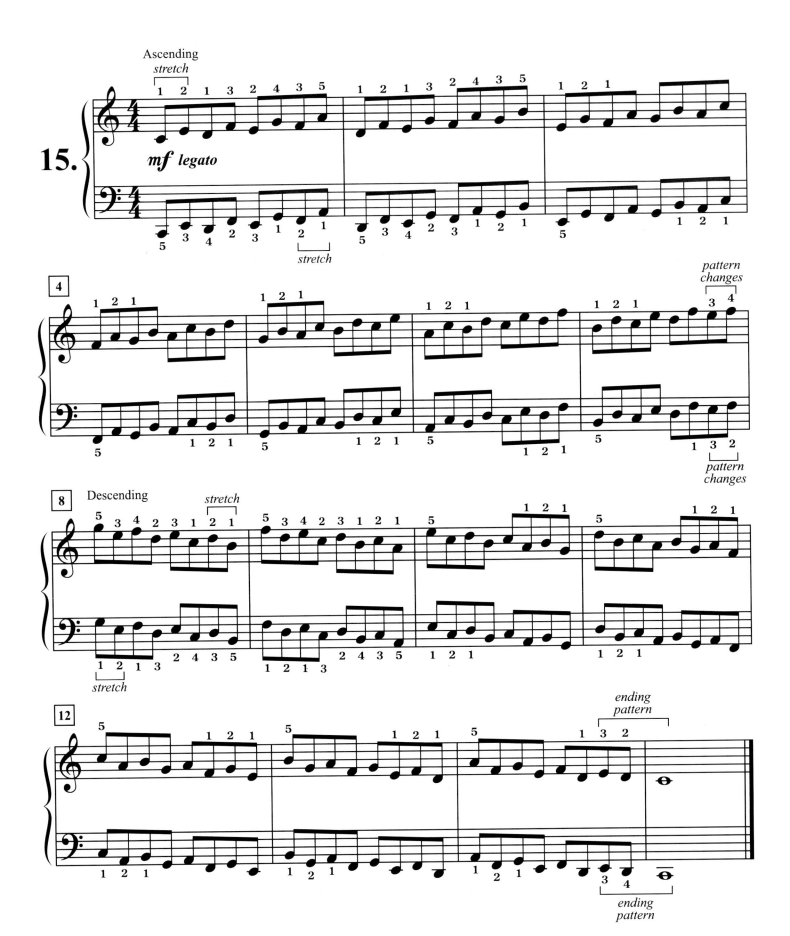

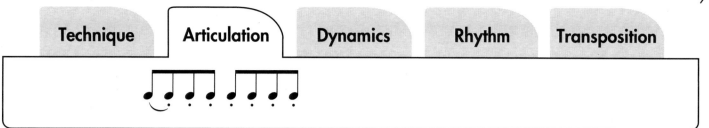

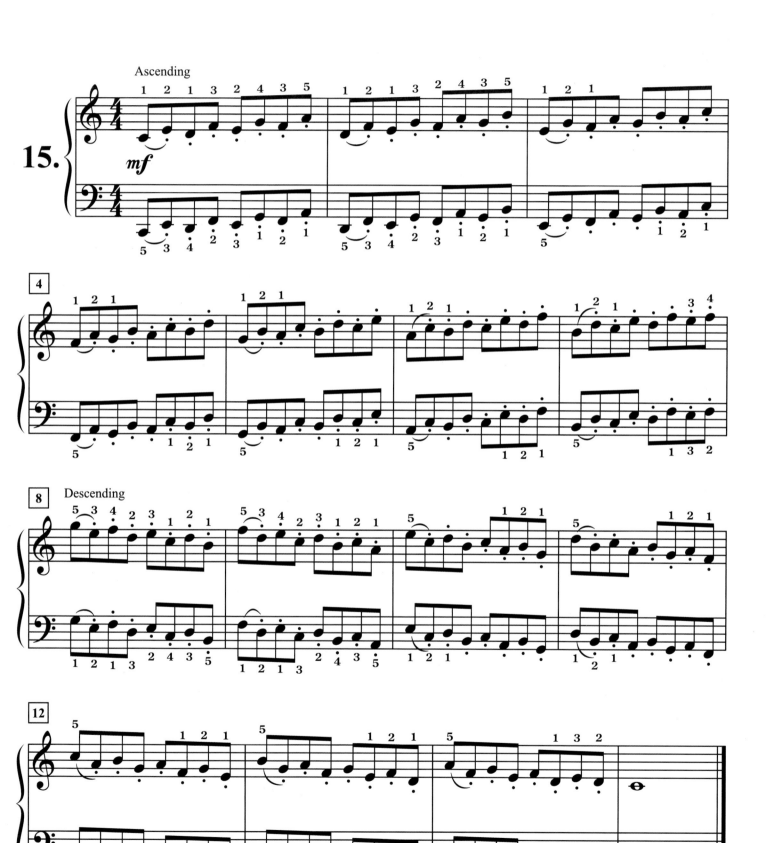

| Technique | Articulation | Dynamics | Rhythm | Transposition |

cresc. poco a poco

dim. poco a poco

15.

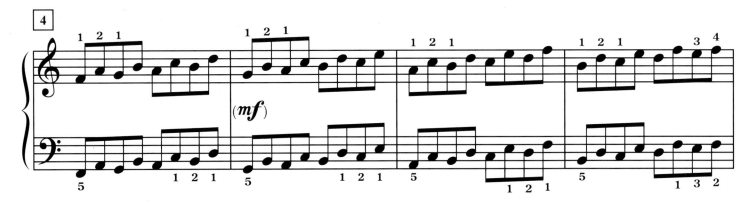

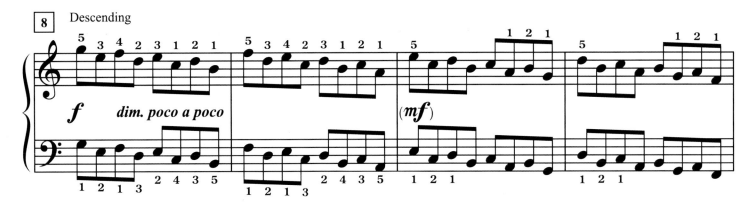

Technique **Articulation** **Dynamics** **Rhythm** **Transposition**

Key of A Major
Remember F-sharp, C-sharp, and G-sharp.

15.

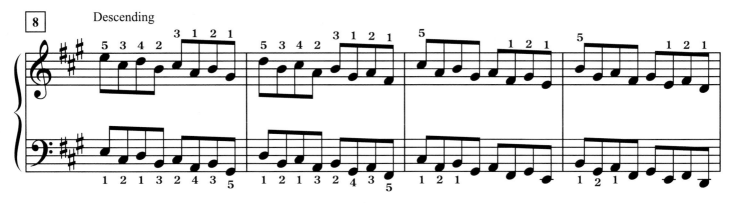

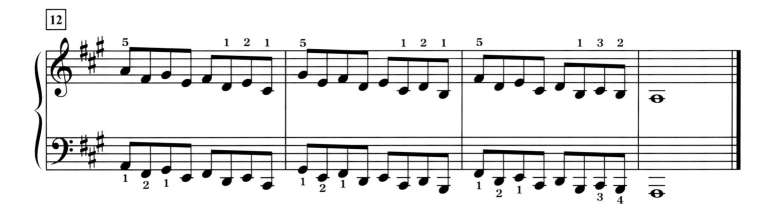

- RH: When *ascending* (mm. 1–7), gently stretch between fingers 3 and 5. When *descending* (mm. 8–15), gently stretch between fingers 2 and 1.
- LH: When *ascending* (mm. 1–7), gently stretch between fingers 3 and 1. When *descending* (mm. 8–15), gently stretch between fingers 1 and 3.

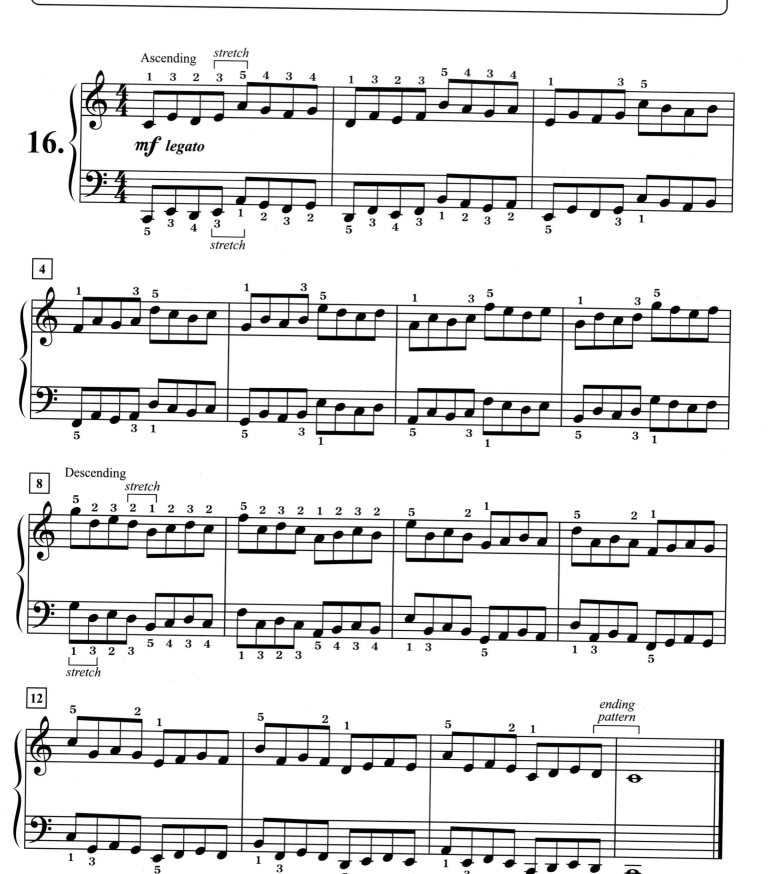

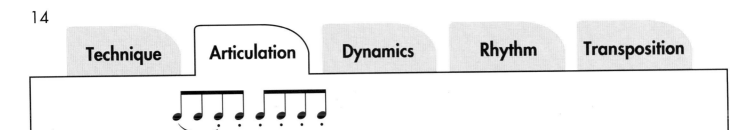

Technique | Articulation | **Dynamics** | Rhythm | Transposition

crescendo
diminuendo

16.

Ascending

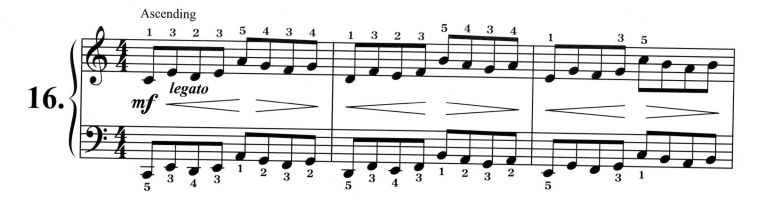

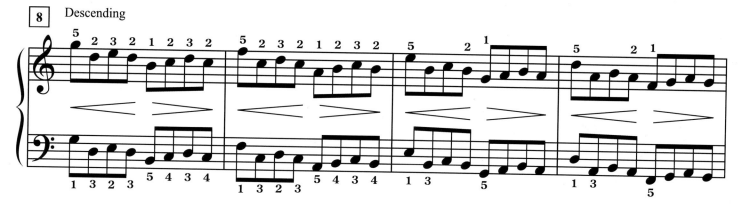

Descending

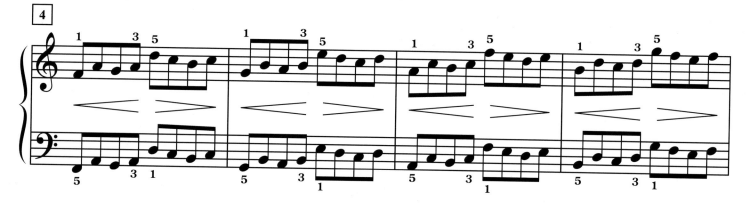

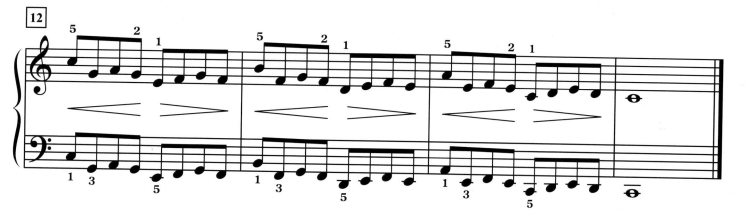

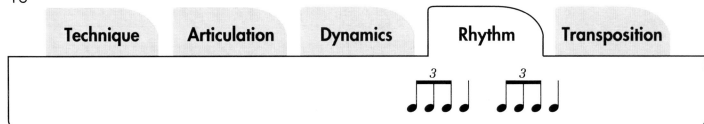

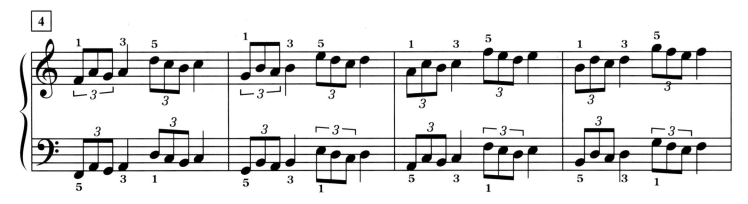

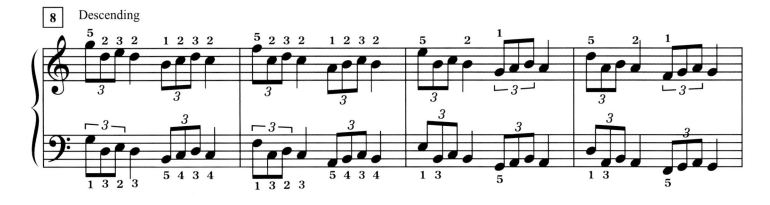

Technique	Articulation	Dynamics	Rhythm	Transposition

Key of E-flat Major
Remember B-flat, E-flat, and A-flat.

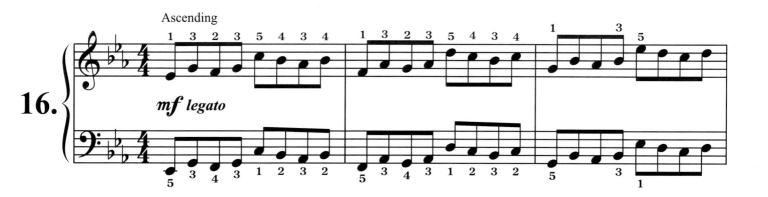

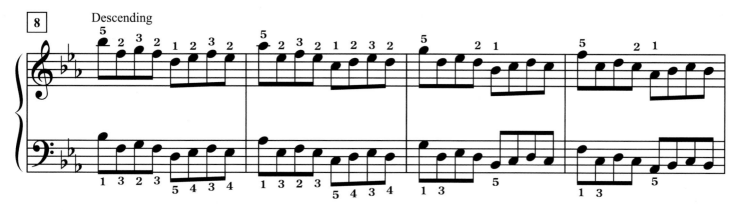

Technique	Articulation	Dynamics	Rhythm	Transposition

- RH: When *ascending* (mm. 1–7), gently stretch between fingers 1 and 2, fingers 2 and 4, and fingers 4 and 1. When *descending* (mm. 8–15), gently stretch between fingers 5 and 3, fingers 3 and 2, and fingers 1 and 5.

- LH: When *ascending* (mm. 1–7), gently stretch between fingers 5 and 4, fingers 4 and 2, and fingers 2 and 5. When *descending* (mm. 8–15), gently stretch between fingers 1 and 2 and fingers 5 and 1.

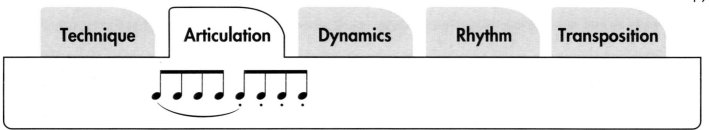

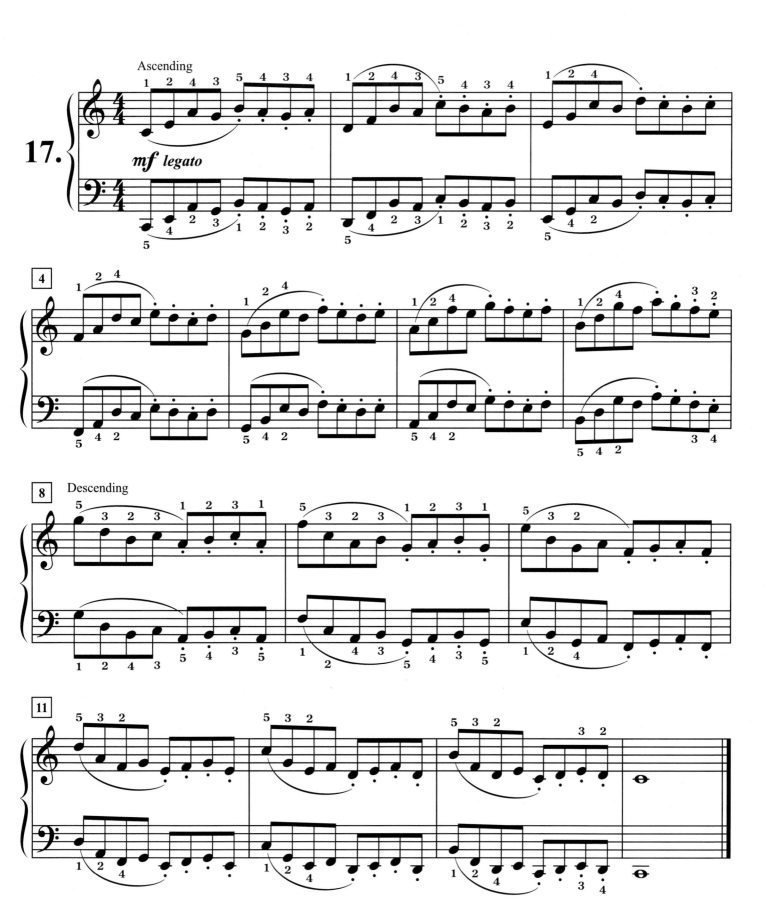

Technique   **Articulation**   **Dynamics**   **Rhythm**   **Transposition**

crescendo

diminuendo

17.

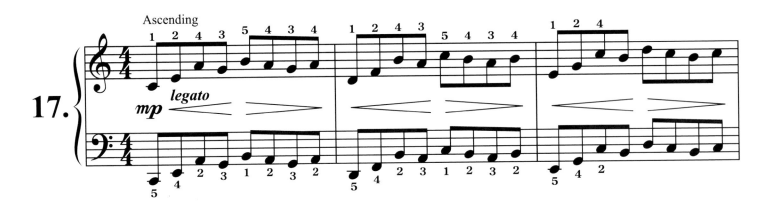

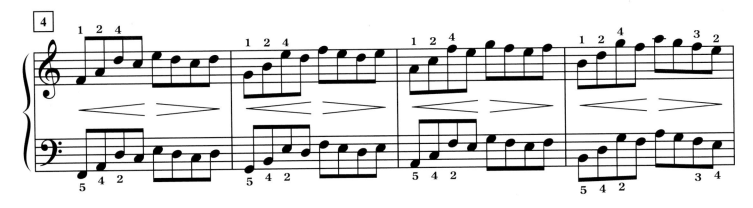

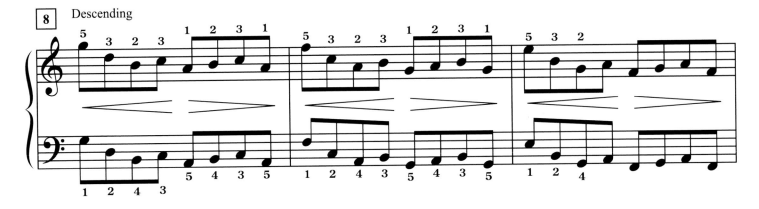

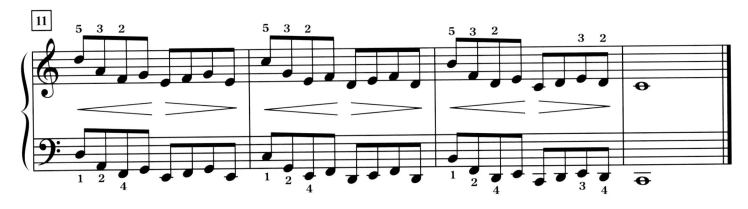

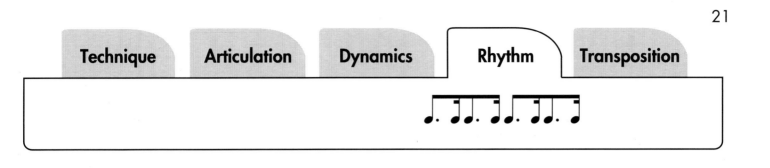

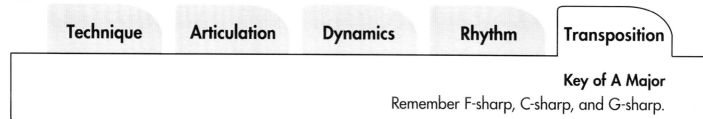

Key of A Major
Remember F-sharp, C-sharp, and G-sharp.

| Technique | Articulation | Dynamics | Rhythm | Transposition |

- RH: When *ascending* (mm. 1–7), gently contract the hand between fingers 3 and 1. When *descending* (mm. 8–15), gently contract the hand between fingers 3 and 5.
- LH: When *ascending* (mm. 1–7), gently contract the hand between fingers 3 and 5. When *descending* (mm. 8–15), gently contract the hand between fingers 3 and 1.

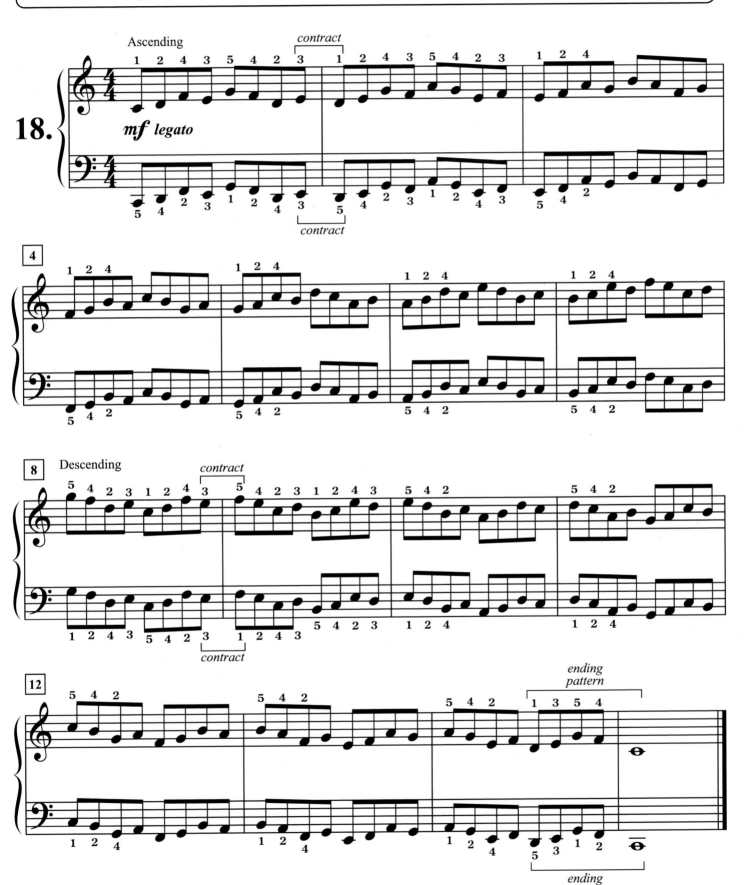

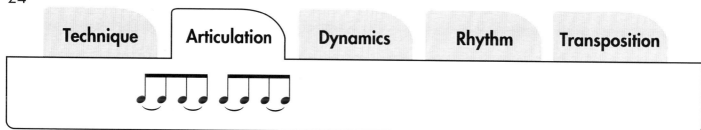

18.

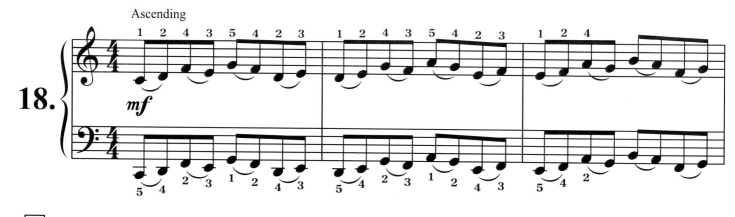

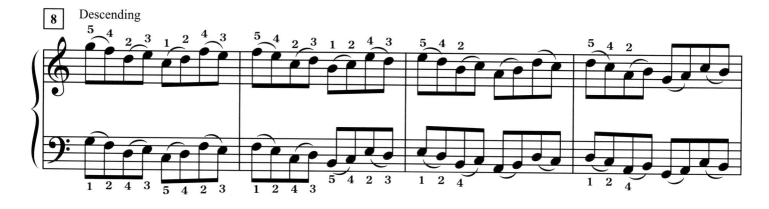

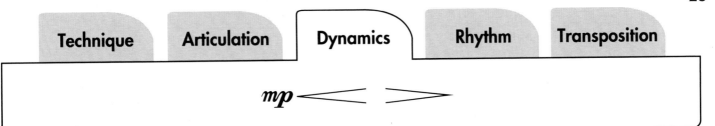

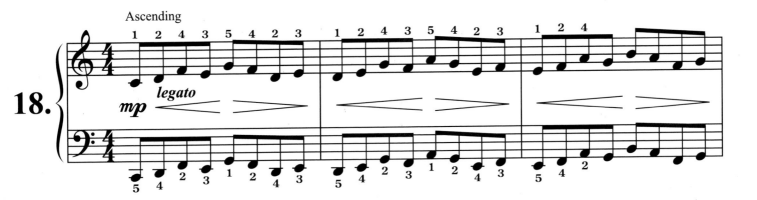

18. Ascending

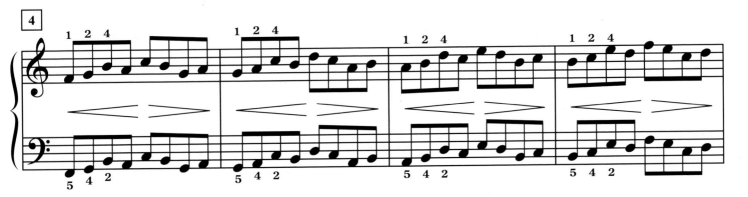

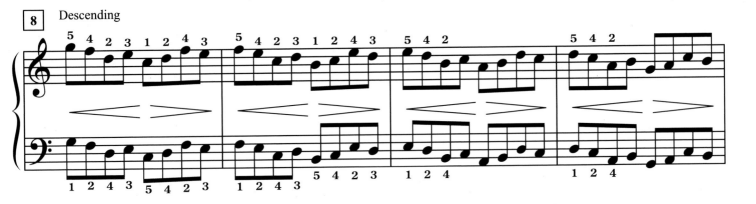

Descending

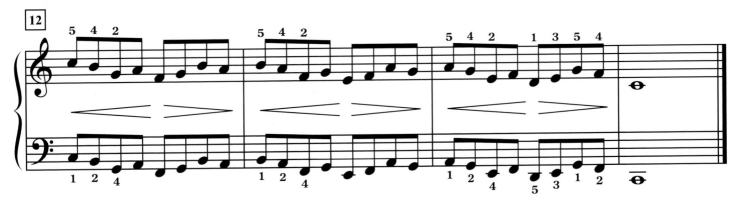

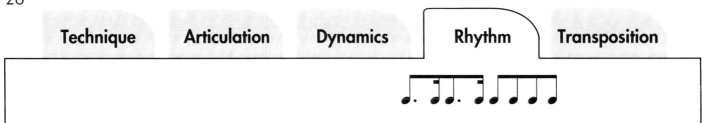

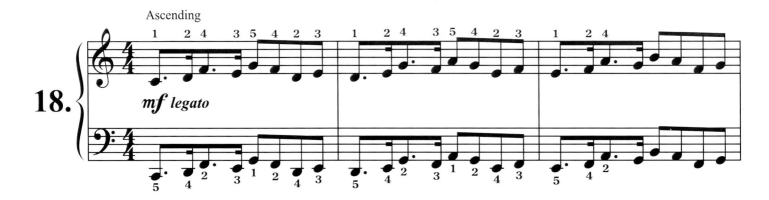

Technique	Articulation	Dynamics	Rhythm	Transposition

Key of E-flat Major
Remember B-flat, E-flat, and A-flat.

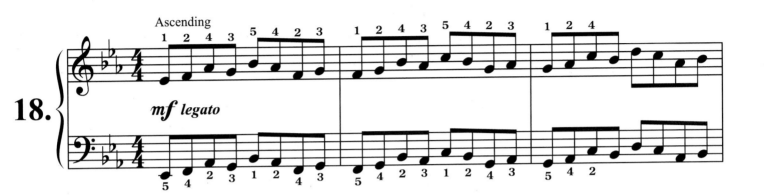

Technique **Articulation** **Dynamics** **Rhythm** **Transposition**

- Gently stretch for the interval of a 6th.
- Keep the wrist relaxed throughout.

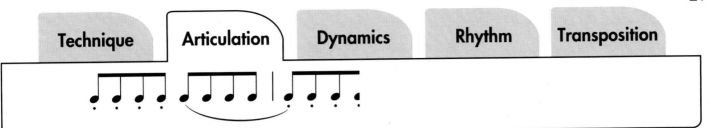

Technique | Articulation | **Dynamics** | Rhythm | Transposition

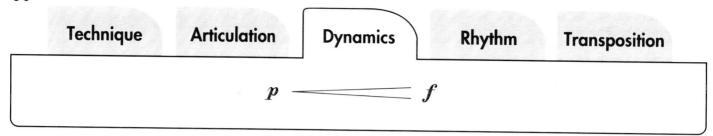

p ⸺⟨ f

❜ This marking indicates to lift the hands and take a short amount of time to prepare for p ⸺⟨ .

19.

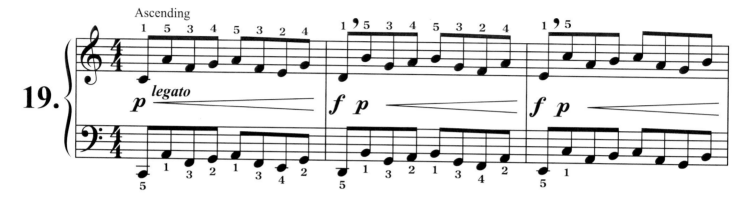

Ascending

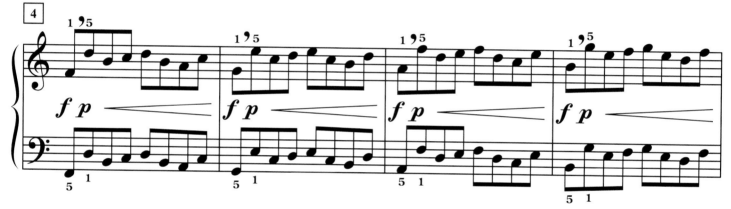

4

8 Descending

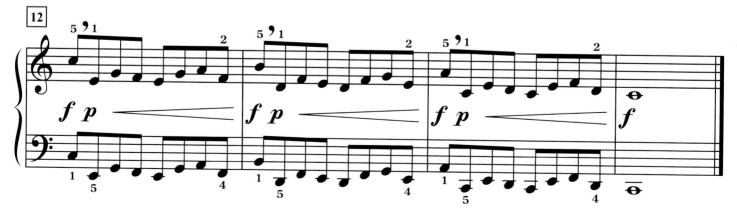

12

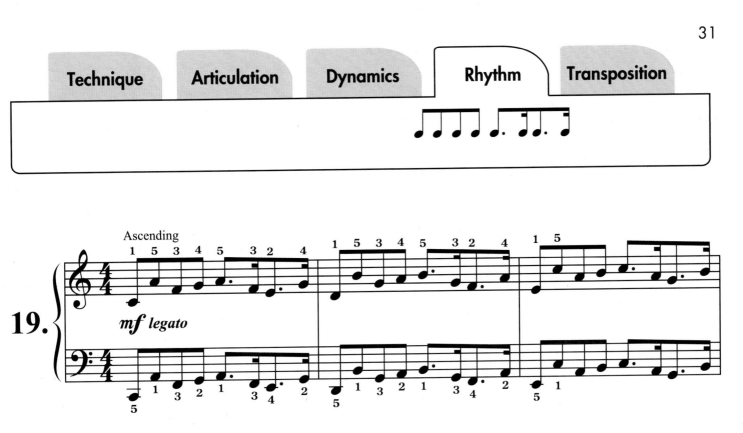

Technique **Articulation** **Dynamics** **Rhythm** **Transposition**

Key of A Major
Remember F-sharp, C-sharp, and G-sharp.

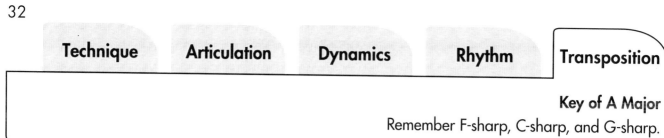

19.

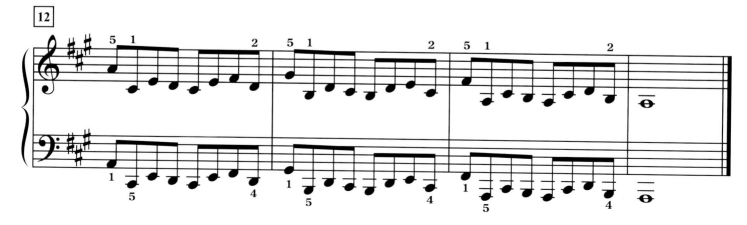

Technique	Articulation	Dynamics	Rhythm	Transposition

- Gently stretch the hand on beats 1 and 2 of each measure.
- When *descending* (mm. 9–17), gently stretch for the interval of a 7th.
- Gently rock the hand and wrist using a small motion on the last four notes of each measure.

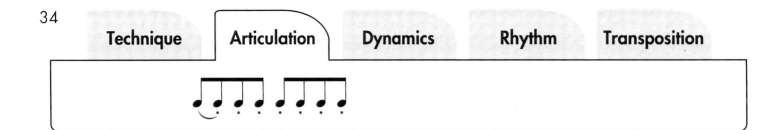

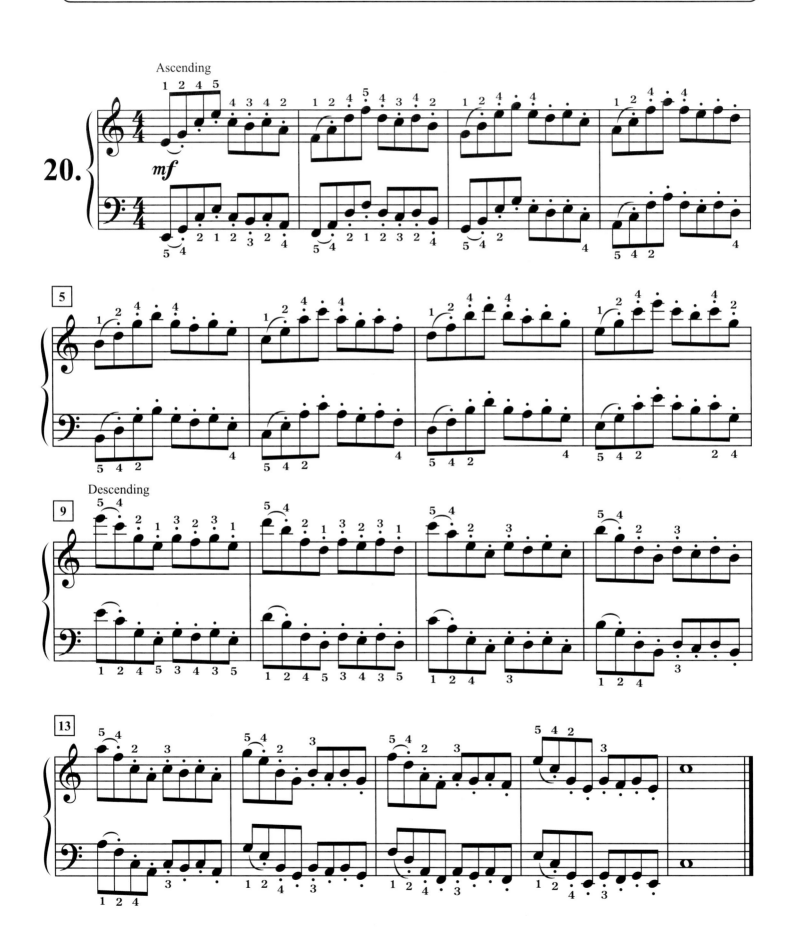

cresc. poco a poco

dim. poco a poco

Technique　　**Articulation**　　**Dynamics**　　**Rhythm**　　**Transposition**

swing style

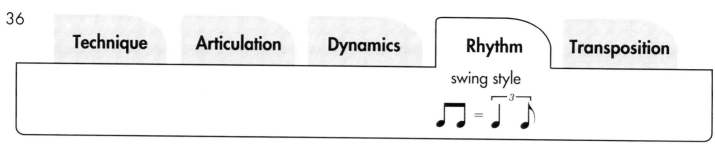

20.　*mf legato*

Ascending

5

Descending

9

13

Technique   Articulation   Dynamics   Rhythm   **Transposition**

Key of E-flat Major
Remember B-flat, E-flat, and A-flat.

Glossary: Harmonic Minor Scales Scales (one octave)

In the harmonic minor scale, the seventh scale degree is raised one half step.

A Minor (no sharps or flats)

E Minor (1 sharp—F♯)

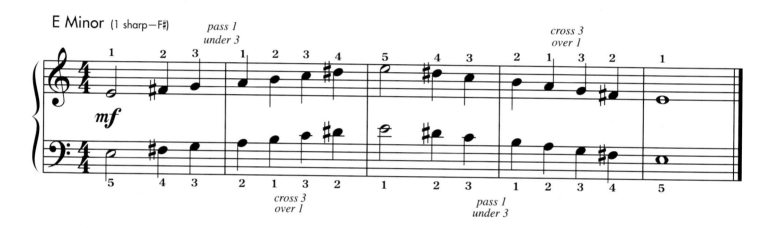

B Minor (2 sharps—F♯, C♯)

F♯ Minor (3 sharps—F♯, C♯, G♯)

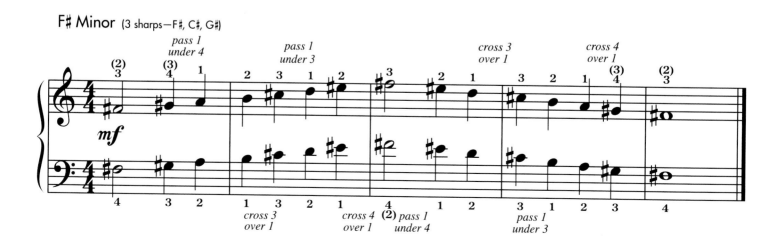

C# Minor (4 sharps—F#, C#, G#, D#)

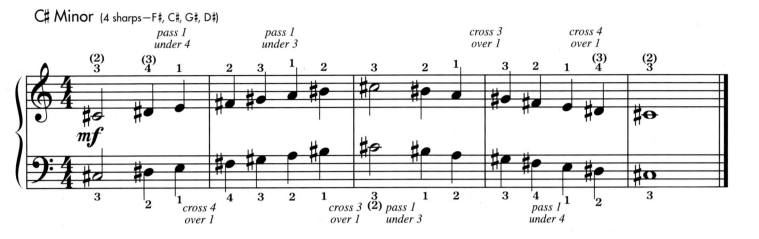

G# Minor (5 sharps—F#, C#, G#, D#, A#)

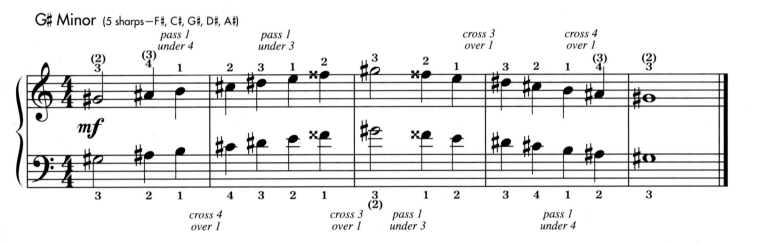

E♭ Minor* (6 flats—B♭, E♭, A♭, D♭, G♭, C♭)

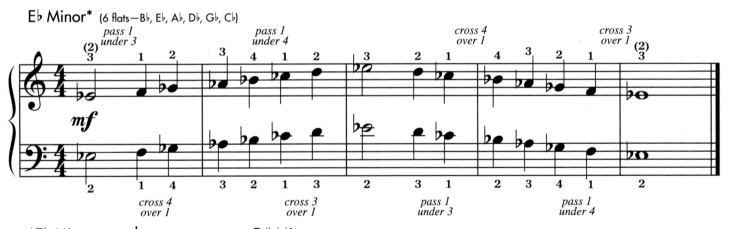

*E♭ Minor uses the same notes as D# Minor (6 sharps—F#, C#, G#, D#, A#, E#)

B♭ Minor (5 flats—B♭, E♭, A♭, D♭, G♭)

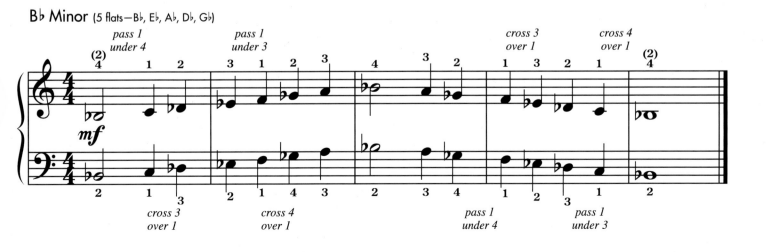

F Minor (4 flats—B♭, E♭, A♭, D♭)

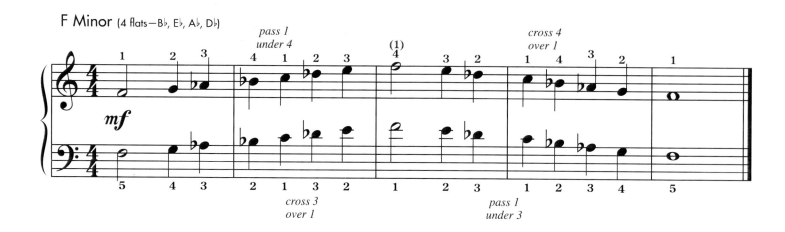

C Minor (3 flats—B♭, E♭, A♭)

G Minor (2 flats—B♭, E♭)

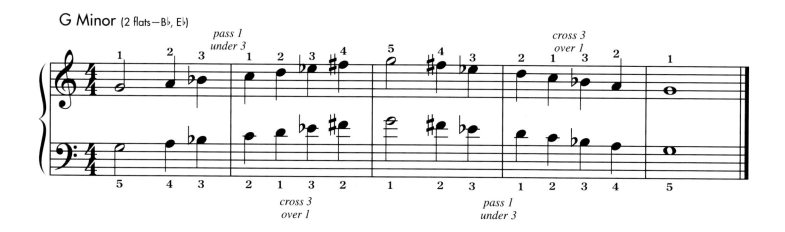

D Minor (1 flat—B♭)

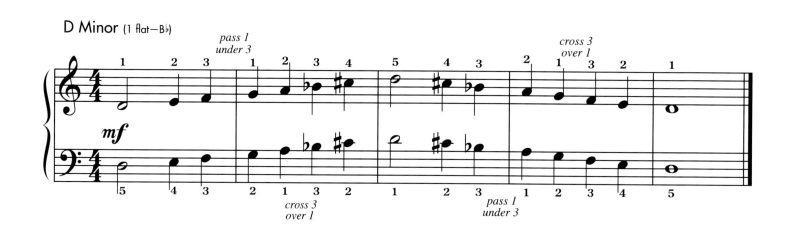